Print
Play

Print
Play

Screen printing inspiration
for your life and home

Jessie Wright & Lara Davies

hardie grant books

Contents

Single colour stencil printing 45

Printing on paper 111

Printing on wood 131

Printing on corkboard 143

Hello!

We are Jess and Lara, the girls from Home-Work Screen Printing. We're OBSESSED with print, pattern and colour, and are so excited to meet you and start you on your own screen printing adventure. Just think of us as your one-stop screen printing coaches and cheerleaders all rolled into one!

We've been designing, printing and teaching together since 2009. But before that, Jess trained as a graphic designer and was deep in the corporate world designing prints for big brands, while Lara went to art school where she majored in drawing. After university, Lara taught textile design and then worked as a freelance print designer for fashion labels, which was when our paths crossed. Our different skills and backgrounds make for the perfect mix of art and design.

When we joined forces to start a textile studio and school, we fell in love with sharing our processes and knowledge with our students – so much so that we decided to write this book, to inspire you to start your own screen printing journey.

Here you'll find 24 fun and creative projects, ranging from very easy to hard (we have included a difficulty rating for each project to help you find your way). So, whether you are an absolute beginner or a screen printing pro, we hope you can find a project in *Print Play* to get you excited!

Screen printing

101

Essentials and basics

What is screen printing?

Screen printing is a very old method of printing – the technique actually dates back to the 18th century, so it's officially old school! The screen printing process involves passing ink through a mesh screen that has been stretched on a frame. A stencil is applied to this frame, which allows patterns and images to be printed onto various surfaces – most commonly fabric and paper. Screen printing is SO easy to do at home, and everything you need is readily found at most art stores. Once you have assembled your screen printing kit (page 12), the printing possibilities are endless.

Your screen printing kit

These are the essential items you'll need to start printing. When we talk about your 'screen printing kit' in the materials list for each project, this is what we are referring to.

1. Pencil

ALWAYS use a pencil to draw on your stencil paper. NEVER use a pen or marker – it will bleed onto your fabric and make you sad.

2. Stencil paper

Stencil paper (also called 'easy cut' or 'Yupo' paper) is a thin, strong plastic that has no grain. It is super easy to cut and lasts forever. You want the stencil paper to be as thin as possible; we don't recommend using acetate or anything too thick. It's also a good idea to have regular drawing paper on hand to map out your designs before you transfer them onto the stencil paper.

3. Light box

A light box is a portable box with a neon tube inside it, and a clear surface. The illuminated surface makes it easy to transfer your design onto the stencil paper. These are sold at art and photographic supply stores. Alternatively, use a brightly lit window when transferring (or tracing) your designs onto stencil paper. Attach the drawing to the window with masking tape, so it doesn't move while you're tracing over it.

4. Scalpel

You'll need one of these to cut all the fine detail in your stencils.

5. Cutting mat

These are used to protect your tabletop when cutting stencils. We recommend using a self-healing mat, and one that's A2 size or bigger will make your life easier.

6. Screen

We prefer screens with aluminium frames, but you can also find screens with wooden frames. Screens are available in many sizes, so pick one that suits your needs (we suggest an A4 to get started).

To print onto fabric you want to make sure your mesh is 43T; to print onto paper you'll want 100T. 43T means that the mesh will allow MORE ink through and 100T means LESS ink. Back in the day, screens were made from silk, but most screens today are made from nylon mesh.

7. Tapes

You'll need to use tape on your screen. We use packing tape to make an 'ink well' (page 17), and masking tape to attach the stencil to the screen.

8. Squeegee

This is used to push the ink through the screen. Make sure that the rubber is quite flexible, and choose one that suits the size of your screen.

9. Ink

This is the fun part! There are so many types of ink (see pages 27–9 for everything you need to know). Save any clean plastic containers and use them for mixing and storing your inks.

10. Spatula

Have a few on hand to mix inks, apply the ink to your screen and to get into all the nooks and crannies during the clean up.

11. Hair dryer

You can leave your prints to air-dry or use a hair dryer to speed things up – this is useful when printing several layers. You can also use a hair dryer to dry your stencils and screen (page 19).

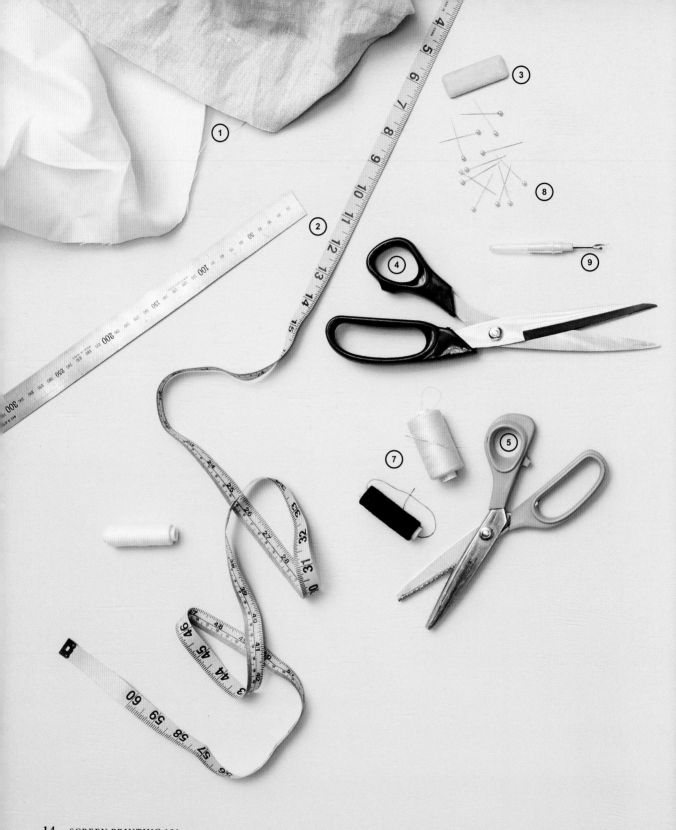

Extra things you may need

1. Cotton and linen fabric
We find that natural fibres are easiest to print on.

2. Tape measure and steel ruler
As the saying goes: measure twice, cut once.

3. Tailor's chalk
Used for making temporary measurements or markings on fabric. These marks are easily removed by light brushing or washing. You can use any colour; we like pastel yellow or pink.

4. Scissors
Make sure they are sharp. This will make cutting your fabric an absolute pleasure.

5. Pinking shears
These zigzag beauties are handy to stop your fabric from fraying.

6. Sewing machine
Dust off that old machine and get ready to sew. You might also need some sewing needles, for hand sewing the fiddly bits.

7. Thread
Pick out colours that match your fabric.

8. Pins
A great excuse to use that cute pincushion.

9. Stitch unpicker
You may need this to unpick sections of thread.

Basic printing step-by-step

Making your stencil

1 Plan and draw your design onto paper. Remember that when creating a stencil you can't have shapes floating inside other shapes; you will need a separate stencil for each layer.

2 Make sure your stencil fits the size of the screen. Place your design over a light box or attach it to a window, and transfer (trace) the design onto stencil paper. ONLY use a pencil when tracing on stencil paper. If you use a pen or marker, the ink will bleed onto your fabric.

3 Place the stencil paper on the cutting mat and use the scalpel to cut out your design. When cutting straight lines, it can be handy to use a metal ruler to keep your lines straight. Your stencil is ready to be printed.

It's all about the preparation

1 Iron your fabric well. Some fabrics need to be pre-washed so they become more absorbent, but most fabrics, including calico, cotton and linen, generally don't need pre-washing. If printing onto wood, corkboard or paper, there is no preparation needed; simply lay it flat on the work surface.

2 Prepare your screen by sticking packing tape to the front (flat side) of the screen to create a border. This makes space at the top, bottom and sides of the screen and is where the ink will start and finish; we call this the 'ink well'. You should only attach tape and stencils to the front of your screen – you want to keep the back as smooth and uninterrupted as possible.

3 Attach your stencil to the front of the screen using two pieces of masking tape. Masking tape is easy to remove when wet, so it will not damage your stencil.

4 Make sure that the stencil overlaps the frame of tape around your screen. Hold the screen up to the light to make sure there is no exposed mesh other than your design, and adjust the stencil or add more packing tape if needed.

Let the printing begin!

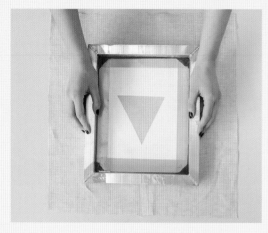

1   Place your screen front-side down on the surface you're printing onto.

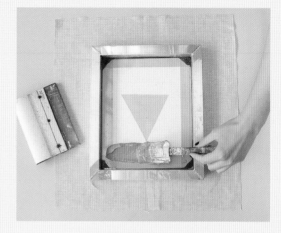

2   Use a spatula to spread a generous amount of ink in the ink well above your design. Hold the screen with one hand (or get a friend to hold it for you) so it doesn't move while you print.

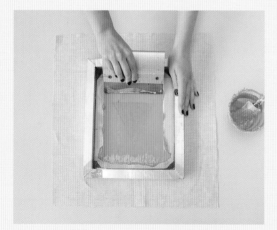

3   Position the squeegee on a 45-degree angle above your design and pull the ink down the screen. Don't apply too much pressure – only use the weight of the squeegee. This is called a FLOOD STROKE; it ensures that your design will get sufficient ink. Now it's time to apply pressure. Using that same 45-degree angle, give the squeegee three hard PULLS across the screen, keeping an even pressure from top to bottom. This process is slightly different for paper, cork and wood (see the relevant projects).

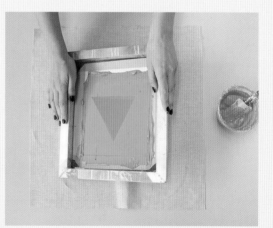

4   Remove the screen from the print by laying one hand flat on one side of the screen and using the other hand to lift the screen up, almost like opening a book. It is best to prop the screen up off the table using a block of wood or a roll of tape until you're ready to clean it.

I have a print ... now what?

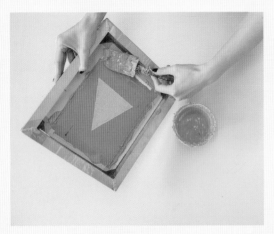

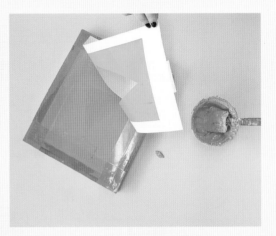

1 Now comes the clean up. Carefully use the spatula to scrape all the excess ink back into the ink pot.

2 Remove the stencil and wash off the ink residue. Allow the stencil to air-dry or carefully dry using a hair dryer.

3 Wash out the screen in running water, making sure you get into all the nooks and crannies. It's important to wash out your screen reasonably quickly – if you leave it too long, the ink will dry in the screen. Once clean, allow the screen to dry. If you opt to use a hair dryer, take care: if the hair dryer gets too close to the screen mesh, the heat can burn a hole in it. If washing the screen between stencils, make sure the screen is completely dry before using it again.

4 Either allow your print to air-dry or, if you're printing on fabric, wood or cork, speed up the process by using a hair dryer. It's important that you keep the hair dryer moving so nothing burns. You can check if your print is dry by lightly pressing a fingertip onto the printed area. If it's dry, no ink will appear on your finger (be careful not to smudge the printed area in case it is still wet).

When can I start using my printed fabric?

Before you use your fabric you need to HEAT SET it. This means that you need to use a heat source to cure the ink onto the fabric. The easiest way to do this is with an iron (the heat from a hair dryer isn't enough).

1 Put your iron on the cotton setting. Don't use steam, as the fabric can't be exposed to water until it has been heat set.

2 Get an old tea towel (or similar) and lay it over your print so you're not ironing directly onto the fabric.

3 Iron the print for at least 5 minutes, but keep the iron moving – you don't want to burn your design.

4 Once you have heat set your print, you can then launder the fabric as usual.

Uh-oh, something went wrong ... troubleshooting guide

When you learn any new skill, there are bound to be a few disasters. Here are a few of the most common ones and how to fix them.

My print has a 'double effect'

This means that your screen has moved during the printing process. You will probably have some ink on the front of the screen, so you'll need to wash and dry the screen and make sure that it is secure during printing.

My print is perfect at the top but hasn't come through at the bottom

This is very common. People often use a LOT of pressure at the top of their print but then less at the bottom. The solution to this is to SLOW DOWN and make sure you're using an even pressure from top to bottom.

My print has bled over all the edges

This means that you have added too much ink or done too many pulls and the ink had nowhere else to go, so it bled underneath the stencil instead of absorbing into the printing surface. Try using less pulls and less ink.

There is a line at the side of my print

This means that there is a gap between the stencil and the frame of packing tape, so some of the mesh has been left exposed. Just cover the exposed mesh with some extra tape and keep printing.

My print is unclear and 'ghosty'

You either need more ink or more pressure. Remember to do your flood stroke! Possibly the ink isn't making it through the screen, so you need to push harder.

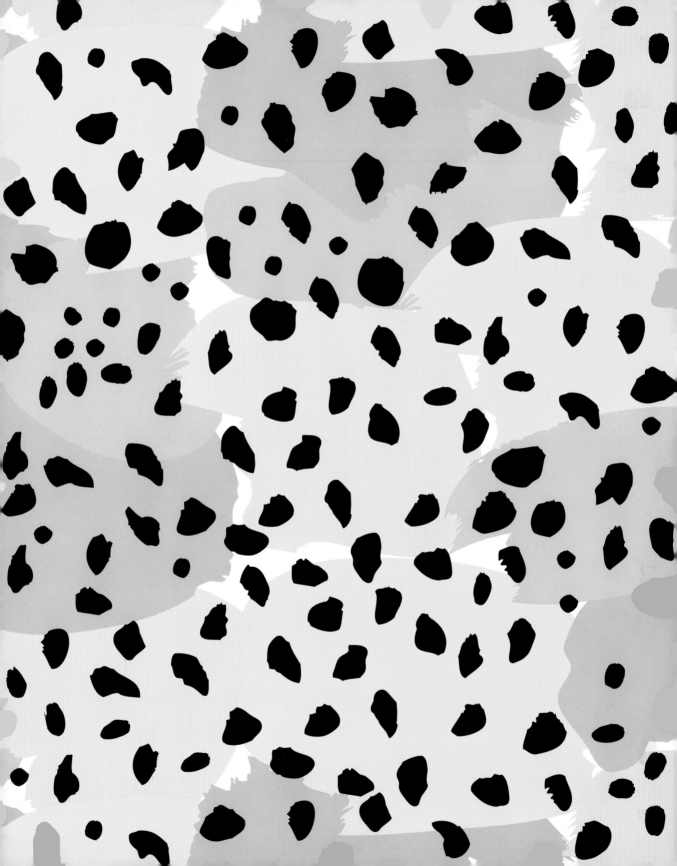

Ink,

colour and pattern

Let's talk about ink

There are different types of inks: inks for printing onto light and dark fabrics, inks in metallics and neon colours, and even inks that glow in the dark.

You can buy screen printing ink from a good art store or textile supplier. We print only with water-based screen printing ink that is non-toxic and easy to clean up with water (we don't want anything that requires harmful chemicals in the cleaning process). This kind of ink is perfect for printing with at home.

Before you head into the store to buy your ink, you should already have a clear idea of what type of surface you want to print on and the type of printing effect you'd like to achieve. All screen printing ink colours come in two variations: transparent and opaque. So, on the shelves you'll see two types of bright scarlets, two types of lemon yellow and so on. And because some ink brands use different words or terms to describe transparent and opaque inks, it's always best to check with the art store employee that the ink you're buying is the most suitable one for your project. It can get a little confusing, but once you figure it out, it's a breeze!

Types of screen printing inks

Transparent

This type of ink is mostly used on light-coloured fabric, as the transparent ink allows the colour of the fabric to show through – so colours appear brighter on white fabric and more earthy when used on a natural-coloured linen.

When you print transparent colours over the top of each other they form new shades. For example, if you print a transparent yellow over blue, you'll get a shade of green. Printing transparent black ink onto a natural linen will give you a dense coverage, but printing with the same colour onto dark fabric can be disappointing – the print will appear as a faint 'film' on the fabric.

After heat setting, transparent inks are soft to touch and appear a part of the fabric – the ink generally tends to permeate through to the back of the fabric.

Opaque

This type of ink is designed to block out whatever colour or fabric is underneath. Opaque inks are generally used to print onto dark fabrics or to achieve bold, blocky colours.

When you print with opaque ink, the ink looks and feels different to printing with a transparent one. Opaque ink is thick (heavy) and looks a lot like cupcake frosting. All opaque colours have an element of white in them to enable the colours to block out whatever is underneath. This means that the colours have a different appearance to their transparent brothers and sisters.

Neon

Neon inks are so much fun to work with. You can either use them straight from the tub, which will give you the classic '80s eye-watering brights, or you can mix them with some opaque white to create our favourite hybrid – the PASTEL NEON. Pastel neon gives you the best of both worlds: you get the bright pop of the neon but it's a little softer on your eyeballs.

Metallic

Metallic inks usually come in gold, silver and bronze. These inks have a metallic, slightly pearlescent finish, which can add a bit of sparkle to your designs.

Foiling

To be clear, when printing with gold foil what you're actually printing with is foiling glue. The metallic foil effect is created after the glue has dried. Foil printing glue is a thick, stinky substance and is used in the same way that you'd use ink in regular screen printing. Once the glue has dried, a sheet of metallic foil is placed over the glue and pressure is applied. The backing sheet is then peeled off, leaving the metallic foil sticking to the glued areas of your design.

Ink for printing on paper

You can print onto paper using a 'screen printing paste' mixed with acrylic paint. The paste has the consistency of hair gel. Mix small amounts of acrylic paint and paste, and then use it to print. This is a great way to make a huge variety of colours using paints you already have. If you're buying paints to make prints on paper, remember the colour vibrancy and depth will depend on the amount of pigment the paint has.

You CAN use fabric screen printing ink on paper as long as the paper weight is more than 200 gsm. Fabric screen printing ink has a high moisture content; if you use it to print onto regular cartridge paper, the paper will warp.

Home-Work hot tips

- As a good starting point, we suggest the following basic range of colours:
  Red warm (transparent)
  Yellow cool (transparent)
  Blue cool (transparent)
  Black (transparent)
  White (opaque)

- You can mix transparent and opaque inks together to utilise the best properties of both inks. We love making pastel colours by mixing opaque white with neon transparent inks.

- We generally use transparent black ink as it has a nice 'handle' when printed. Because it is a dark colour, it still gives full blockout.

- To make the perfect white for printing, we mix 50 per cent opaque white ink with 50 per cent transparent white. This 50/50 white gives the perfect coverage without drying too quickly in your screen mid print (transparent ink dries slower in the screen than opaque ink).

- Store your ink in a cool place away from direct sunlight to ensure it has a long life.

Pick a colour, any colour

One of the most enjoyable decisions you'll get to make during the design process is what colour or colour combinations to use in your print. But this can also be a little tricky. A good way to start is to print your first design in a few different colours to see just how much your choice of colour can affect the look and feel of the same design. Being both designer and printer means that you will also need to consider your fabric type and colour when choosing that perfect shade.

Things to consider when choosing colours

Contrast

To achieve a high-impact print you need to choose a high-contrast colour combination: for example, printing black onto a white surface, or opaque white onto a black surface.

Colour combinations

We are all for crazy colour combinations, and colour is such a subjective thing. Pull out some of your favourite outfits or homewares and use them as a jumping off point for colour combinations you might be drawn to.

Creating a palette

We love creating a colour palette. Grab an image that you love, perhaps from a book or magazine, and pick out some of the key colours. Ta-da – you've created a colour palette! Another great way to do this is to collect some paint swatches from your local hardware store. These can be handy to mix and match different colours and to create your own unique palettes.

Colour theory basics

Primary colours

These colours are red, yellow and blue. In traditional colour theory, primary colours are the three pigment colours that can't be created by any combination of other colours. All other colours are derived from these key three.

Secondary colours

These colours are purple, orange and green. They are the colours formed by mixing the primary colours.

Tertiary colours

These colours are yellow-orange, red-orange, red-purple, blue-purple, blue-green and yellow-green. They are formed by mixing a primary and a secondary colour.

Tint

A tint is the mixture of a colour with white, which boosts the lightness. Pink and light blue are examples of tints.

Shade

A shade is the mixture of a colour with black, which decreases lightness. Mustard, maroon and navy are examples of shades.

Tone

A tone is created by mixing a colour with grey.

Our favourite colour palettes

These are four of our favourite colour palettes that we find ourselves coming back to time and time again.

Blue

Lara: This is my favourite colour palette. I love every shade of blue and I always find myself drawn to this colour.

Pink

Jess: This is my favourite colour palette. I've never met a shade of pink that I didn't love – except maybe fuchsia.

Multicolour

Brights and pastels always make a wonderful colour combo! For this palette we used our FAVOURITE loud vintage sweater as inspiration. We love how the lemon yellow and baby pink really soften the bold red, blue and black. Grab your number one piece of colourful clothing and use it to create a palette that you're sure to love.

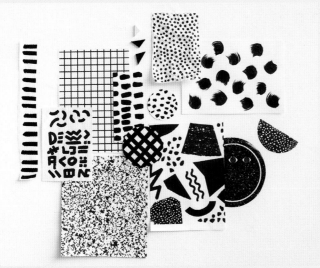

Absence of colour

When in doubt about what colours to use, go for some monochrome magic. Black and white ALWAYS look good together.

Make your mark

Our work is inspired by nature and the objects we see around us. Anyone can learn to screen print, but what we really want you to understand is the importance of design and how to take your design inspiration through to a completed product. To create a new range of patterns we always start with inspiration imagery and go from there.

Here are a few tips to keep in mind when designing your patterns:

- Using a collection of various objects or motifs always looks great. It's also good to draw the same object from a number of different perspectives.

- Simple, bold shapes always work well in a pattern.

- Consider the scale of your pattern design and how this will work on the object you're printing. For example, if you're printing fabric for something small, you might like a smaller and tightly spaced repeated motif so you don't have large empty sections of fabric.

As individuals we each have our own style and aesthetic, but after working together for many years we've developed a unique style that clearly says 'Jess and Lara'. The information on the following pages explains our creative processes and how we work together to create our Home-Work designs, but we encourage you to explore and follow your own design path.

What inspires us?

Jess

I've loved big, bold patterns for as long as I can remember. I've always been drawn to '80s and '90s design – there's something about the bright and playful designs from those decades that make me very happy.

I was raised in a house full of colourful fabric and patterns, and I feel most comfortable surrounded by STUFF. I spend as much time as I can in thrift stores and I get SO much inspiration from the kooky knick-knacks and clothing that I find in them.

I always want to draw a face on everything. Leopard print everything. I worship the style of Aussie design icon Linda Jackson and I NEVER say no to sequins. My aesthetic is definitely not subtle – if it's cute, pink and plastic I'll probably buy it. And plants, lots and lots of plants.

Lara

I am inspired by anything and everything, really! I love drawing and have drawn ever since I could hold a pencil. When I was a kid, the wall in my bedroom was always covered with drawings that inspired me. While the journey started with drawing ballerinas and princess dresses, I eventually moved on to observing the natural world around me. I find so much inspiration in plants and flowers.

I am crazy about patterns, anything from patterns in nature to traditional old wallpapers – there is nothing more pleasing than a pattern!

I hate shopping, but I love collecting objects that have a story and meaning to me. Much of the pottery I own comes from my grandparents' and parents' homes or from potters I admire.

Our design process

1. Inspiration imagery

To create a new range of patterns we always start with inspiration imagery: things such as our own photographs, pictures from books and magazines, postcards, and images we find online. First we'll have a conversation about the look and feel we want to capture; we talk about trends, themes or colours we are currently loving.

2. Inspiration board

We collate a range of objects, images and our own drawings and turn them into an inspiration board (or mood board). This board is where we source the inspiration for our shapes and patterns. For more on how to make an inspiration board, see page 43.

3. Designs and shapes

Lara draws and paints different designs and shapes based on the inspiration board.

4. Print design

Jess takes the drawings and paintings and turns them into a completed print design. As you can see, the process is a very collaborative one!

Creating an inspiration board

Anyone who visits our studio comments on the walls. Our walls are COVERED with images that inspire us. We like to surround ourselves with patterns, shapes and colours that we love.

Whenever we are creating new prints we always create an inspiration board to get started. We gather all the colours, images and items that we are loving and put them all together. You can do this on the computer but we like to do it the old-fashioned way.

Start by gathering any drawings and paintings you've done – they don't have to be perfect. Then gather all the images you've been collecting: magazine pages, fabric samples, postcards, old wrapping paper from the thrift store, photocopies of images from old books, brooches from the flea market, childhood stickers, paint swatches from the hardware store … There are no rules here; just make sure you LOVE them all. Then just start sticking them on the wall – use a board or a big piece of paper if you don't want to stick things directly on the wall.

Once you have created your inspiration wall, stand back and have a good look at it. You should notice a theme emerging. It might be certain colours or motifs that you're drawn to, and this will be the jumping off point for your designs and will give you a clear picture of your design style.

We've created an inspiration board for each of the project chapters in this book, so you can see how our design process works. And, let's be honest, we'll jump at any chance to stick things to the walls!

Single colour
stencil printing

Time to get started on some FRESH PRINTS! We've collected some leaf shapes and some of our favourite colours to inspire the designs in this chapter.

Y'all ready for this?

In this chapter, we start with the basics of how to print single colour designs onto pre-made items using a stencil, as well as how to print and sew a pencil case.

Plants are a huge source of inspiration for us, so we love filling the studio, both inside and out, with lots of pot plants in all shapes and sizes. The beautiful lines and curves of leaves and their simple, graphic shapes are perfect for inspiring a print or pattern. We think plants make EVERY space better.

Tea towels

While drying the dishes is hardly the most exciting thing to do, the humble tea towel happens to be one of the easiest pre-made items for printing on. Tea towels are the perfect canvas for first time printers: they're flat and often blank and are always made from a natural fibre.

Handy hints

- We find natural fibres work best for screen printing. We recommend that you start out printing on cotton and then build up to linen once you become more confident. Cotton is easier to print onto, as linen absorbs a lot of ink. If you're printing onto linen, do a test print on a scrap piece of linen first.

- For best results, iron your fabric before printing.

- Avoid printing on, or too close to, the seam of the tea towel.

- Think about how you position the design on your tea towel so it looks good when flat, as well as hanging on an oven door.

- We recommend you print two tea towels. It's rare that you'll get the first print right, so it's good to have a backup.

You will need

screen printing kit (page 12)
iron
2 blank cotton or linen tea towels
ink in 1 colour

1 Draw your design, transfer it onto stencil paper, then cut your stencil (page 16). The design for this project was inspired by our love of indoor plants.

2 Iron your tea towels and lay them out flat on the work surface. Prepare the screen and attach the stencil to the front (page 17). Get your squeegee and ink ready.

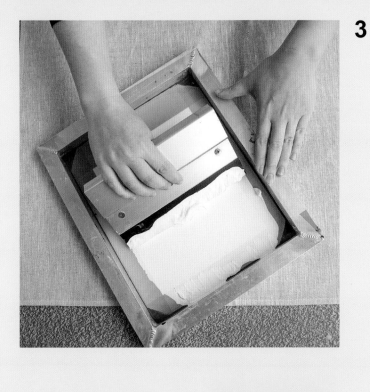

3 Place the screen on top of the first tea towel. Use a spatula to spread a generous amount of ink above your design. Start printing with one flood stroke and then apply pressure during your three hard pulls. Carefully lift up the screen from the fabric (page 18).

4 Place the screen onto other areas of the tea towel, positioning the screen in different directions each time, and repeat the printing process. Do the same with the second tea towel. Once you're done, peel off the stencil and wash it, then wash the screen. Dry the prints completely using a hair dryer (page 19). Heat set your tea towels with an iron (page 20).

Tote bag

DIFFICULTY:
Easy

A wise person once said, 'You can never have too many tote bags.' This is a mantra we live by. Tote bags are an awesome present for your sister, brother, best friend, mum, mother-in-law, your kid's kindergarten teacher, your nan, the sweet old lady down the road who gives you parsley … get the picture? Everyone needs a tote bag, so here is a simple technique to customise your own.

Handy hints

- Avoid printing too close to the straps and seams of your tote. The seams on a tote handle are especially bulky.
- When heat setting the fabric, use your iron on the cotton setting. Remember to turn the steam off, as the fabric can't be exposed to water until it has been heat set.

You will need

screen printing kit (page 12)
iron
blank tote bag in a natural fibre
scrap paper or card
ink in 1 colour

1 Draw your design, transfer it onto stencil paper, then cut your stencil (page 16). We've used our favourite plant in our studio, *Monstera deliciosa*, as inspiration.

2 Prepare the screen and attach the stencil to the front (page 17).

3 Iron your tote bag and lay it out flat on the work surface. Place a piece of scrap paper inside the bag, so the ink doesn't bleed through to the other side. Get your squeegee and ink ready. Place the screen on top of the tote bag. Use a spatula to spread a generous amount of ink above your design (page 18).

4 Start printing with one flood stroke and then apply pressure during your three hard pulls (page 18).

5 Carefully lift up the screen from the fabric (page 18). Peel off the stencil and wash it, then wash the screen. Dry the print completely using a hair dryer (page 19). Heat set your tote bag with an iron (page 20).

Fabric pencil case

This project makes perfect use of all that leftover fabric in your stash. You can breathe new life into basic printed fabric by printing over it with your own designs. We LOVE these pencil cases – they are a lifesaver for people like us who have way too much stuff in our handbags. We have one for pencils, one for dog treats, one for make-up, one for hot sauce sachets … These super cute pencil cases have turned us into the super organised people we always wanted to be!

Handy hints

- We used a vintage striped fabric for our pencil case, but you can use anything you like from your fabric stash.

- It can be fun to juxtapose different prints on top of each other – try a bold geometric print over a traditional floral fabric.

- You can scale up or down to create a series of zipped bags in different sizes, perfect for travelling or organising your life.

- For best results, use a fabric that is made of a natural fibre, such as cotton or linen.

You will need

screen printing kit (page 12)
ruler
iron
40 × 60 cm (16 × 24 in) striped fabric
scissors
ink in 1 colour
sewing machine (with zipper foot) and thread
20 cm (8 in) zipper
pins

1 Draw your design onto paper, making sure it's no bigger than 16 × 26 cm (6¼ × 10¼ in), so it will comfortably fit onto the pencil case. Transfer the design onto stencil paper, then cut your stencil (page 16). We've used a plant leaf as inspiration for our design.

2 Iron your fabric, then cut it in half, so that each piece measures 20 × 30 cm (8 × 12 in). Lay the two pieces of fabric out flat on the work surface, right side up. You will print onto both pieces.

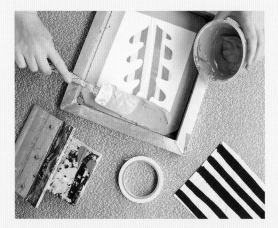

3 Prepare the screen and attach the stencil to the front (page 17). Get your squeegee and ink ready. Spread a generous amount of ink above your design. Start printing with one flood stroke and then apply pressure during your three hard pulls. Carefully lift up the screen (page 18). Repeat with the second piece of fabric. Peel off the stencil and wash it, then wash the screen. Dry the prints using a hair dryer (page 19). Heat set the fabric (page 20).

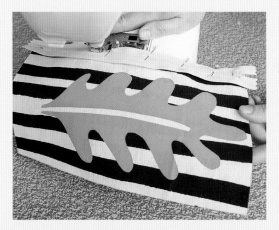

4 Put the zipper foot on your sewing machine. Take your first piece of fabric, printed side up, and align the zipper face down on the long edge of the fabric. Pin into place. Position the fabric in the machine with the zipper head towards you and sew along the edge of the zipper until you reach the halfway point. Open up the zipper completely, as the foot cannot go over the zipper head. Sew until you reach the end of the zipper, then sew back and forth to secure the line of stitching. Remove the pins.

5 Place your first piece of fabric on the work surface, making sure the printed side is facing up and the zipper is facing down. Lay the second piece of fabric on top, so the printed sides are facing each other. Pin the free side of the zipper along the edge of the second piece of fabric.

6 Sew along the edge of the zipper until you reach halfway, then open the zipper completely. Continue sewing to the end of the zipper, then sew back and forth to secure the stitching. Your zipper is in place. Remove the pins and use an iron to press open the zipper seams. Position the pieces of fabric with the printed sides together, lining up the edges and zipper ends. Pin into place.

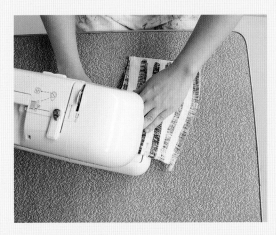

7 Remove the zipper foot from the machine and attach the straight stitch foot. Using a 1 cm (½ in) seam allowance, sew around the sides and base of the pencil case, making sure you backstitch each corner to strengthen it. Trim the edges and cut off any loose threads.

8 Turn the pencil case right way out and push out the corners. Press with a cool iron. Your pencil case is ready to use.

Multicolour

stencil printing

When in doubt, embrace geometric shapes! Here is a selection of some of our go-to shapes that we use to create endless combinations of fun.

Cut loose

We love shopping in thrift stores – we're always on the lookout for anything with a unique shape or interesting pattern or texture. The design inspiration for these projects comes from our collection of quirky objects and shapes. Take a look around your own home with a fresh eye – almost any object will have so much visual information (colour, shape, texture, pattern) to inspire your prints.

This chapter explains the process of multicoloured printing. You may want to revisit the section on Colour (pages 30–5) and come up with some colour combinations before you print, OR you can throw yourself in the deep end and learn by trial and error. Either way, the first thing to consider is how your shapes and colours are going to work together: will your chosen colours match well and will your design elements complement each other? It can be worth using coloured paper to cut out a bunch of shapes and experiment with them until you settle on a design you love!

As this is your first step into multicoloured printing, we've kept the style here fairly loose and unplanned. The idea is to embrace this technique – then, when you're comfortable with it, you can jump into the more planned and precise techniques (for all you control freaks) in later chapters!

Cushion cover

A cushion on your couch or favourite armchair presents a perfect opportunity to add some colour and pattern to your home in a non-committal, easy-to-replace kinda way. And you may have noticed that we are pretty crazy about pattern and colour! We believe a home and its decor should evolve to tell a story over time and these colourful cushions are a great place to start. Inspired by an eclectic mix of random objects from around the studio, this pattern is SO fun to design as well as print.

Handy hints

- Make sure your fabric is washed and ironed before you start printing.

- These instructions are to print one panel of your cushion cover; however, we recommend you cut and print at least two panels at the same time. This ensures you'll always have a 'test' print and then another panel (or more) as your final piece. When printing with lots of stencils, it's a real bummer if you make a mistake on the final layer of your only panel and then lose all your hard work!

You will need

screen printing kit (page 12)
selection of your favourite objects
scissors
1 m (1 yd) fabric in your choice of colour
(this is enough for one complete cushion
plus 1 or 2 spare front panels)
inks in 5 or 6 colours, but it's up to you!
iron
sewing machine and thread
pins
45 × 45 cm (17¾ × 17¾ in) cushion insert

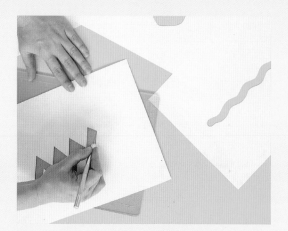

1 On a piece of paper, draw a selection of shapes for the front of your cushion cover. To do this, simply grab some of your favourite objects and trace around them, or draw the shapes freehand if you prefer. Use about eight or nine objects, then choose the shapes you like best. We've chosen some simple graphic shapes.

2 Cut separate stencils for each of your shapes. Some of our cushions (main photo) use more shapes and some use less – it's up to you how many you use. Transfer your design (draw it freehand if you like) onto stencil paper, then cut the stencils using your scalpel and cutting mat (page 16).

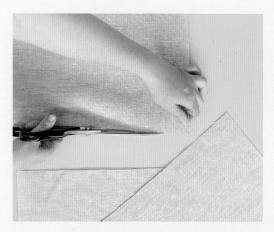

3 Cut a square of fabric measuring 46 × 46 cm (18 × 18 in) – this will be the front panel of your cushion. Cut out two rectangles measuring 33 × 46 cm (13 × 18 in) – these will create the envelope backing of your cushion. Cut one or two extra front panels as backups (see Handy hints).

4 Lay the front panel flat on the work surface, right side up. Prepare the screen and attach the first stencil to the front (page 17). Get your squeegee and ink ready. Place the screen in position, then spread a generous amount of ink above your design. Start printing with one flood stroke and then apply pressure during your three hard pulls. Carefully lift up the screen (page 18).

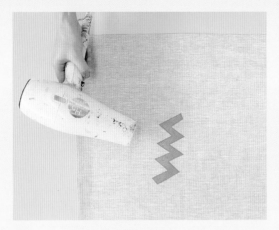

5 Peel off the stencil and wash it, then wash the screen so it's ready for the next print. Make sure the screen is dry before printing your second shape. Dry the first print completely using a hair dryer (page 19).

6 Repeat steps 4–5 for each of your stencils until you have filled your cushion cover with different coloured shapes. Heat set your printed panel with an iron (page 20).

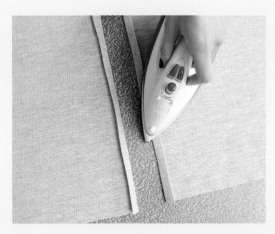

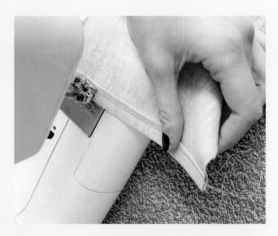

7 Take one of the backing fabric rectangles and lay it right side down. Fold one of the long sides over 1 cm (½ in), then press firmly with the iron. Fold over another 1 cm (½ in) and press firmly with the iron again. Repeat this for the second rectangle.

8 Using the sewing machine, carefully sew along the folded seam on both rectangles. Sew back and forth at the end of each line of stitching to secure them.

9 Place one of the rectangles directly on top of your printed panel, lined up with the left side of the panel and with right sides of the fabric together. Place the second rectangle on top of both panels, right side down and lined up with the right side of the panels. The two rectangles should overlap each other. This will create the envelope opening at the back of the cushion.

10 Pin and then sew around the whole perimeter of the cushion.

11 Cut off any loose threads and clip any excess fabric in the corners.

12 Turn your cushion right side out and press with the iron. Put the cushion insert inside the cover and admire your work!

Beach towel

A bit like its little cousin the tea towel, the beach towel is a vast, flat canvas just begging to be printed on. We've used a Turkish towel for this project, as it has a smoother surface than a traditional terry towelling beach towel, which makes printing a little easier. When designing our prints we went BIG in scale to suit the jumbo size of the towel. Make a splash with your design choices!

Handy hints

- If you're using a towel made from terry towelling, it's best to stick to solid, simple shapes when planning your design – it's nearly impossible to capture fine detail on the rough texture of the towel.
- Avoid printing too close to the edges of the towel.
- This technique works well for hand towels, bath mats and bath towels, too.

You will need

screen printing kit (page 12)
iron
large light-coloured cotton beach towel
inks in 4 colours

1 Draw your design onto a piece of paper. You can sketch out several shapes, then choose the ones you like the best. We've used four big, bold shapes. Transfer the shapes onto stencil paper, then cut your stencils (page 16).

2 Iron your beach towel and lay it out flat. Prepare the screen and attach the first stencil to the front (page 17). Get your squeegee and inks ready. Place the screen in position and spread a generous amount of ink above your design. Start printing with one flood stroke and then apply pressure during your three hard pulls (page 18).

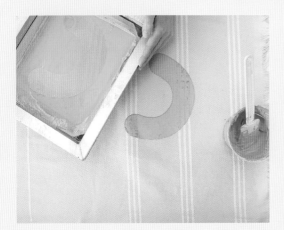

3 Carefully lift up the screen from the fabric and repeat. You can print the same shape a few times in different spots on the towel. Peel off the stencil and wash it, then wash the screen so it's ready for the next print. Make sure the screen is dry before printing the next shape. Use a hair dryer to dry each print on your towel before printing the next one (page 19).

4 Repeat steps 2–3 for each of your stencils, in different colours, until you've filled your towel with shapes. Heat set your towel with an iron (page 20) and you're ready to hit the beach!

Multicolour

registration printing

We are keeping it all lined up in this chapter, with colours and shapes designed to make you smile.

Registration sensation!

Registered printing requires a bit more planning than the random techniques used in previous chapters. The registration technique is perfect for when it's really important that all the printed elements are in the right spot – for example, when printing faces or designs that use lettering. Some people like to register the printing by eye, but when you see the techniques we use you'll see how easy it is to get the perfect print every time!

In this chapter we print a rainbow T-shirt, a modernist wall hanging and a geometric pillowcase. These projects require a bit of planning, so it's important to read through all the instructions before you start.

Rainbow T-shirt

We still get a little thrill every time we spot a rainbow. This magical meteorological phenomenon is the inspiration for our T-shirt print design. It also has the added bonus of requiring lots of gorgeous colours to mix up. We've stuck to a pretty traditional rainbow palette, but it would also look beautiful using different shades of the same colour. Imagine one in shades of pink ... yum!

Handy hints

- You may want to set up multiple T-shirts to print at the one time, depending on how much space you have.

- Each colour in a screen print is a new layer. So, if you're printing two colours you will need two stencils; if you're printing three colours, you will need three stencils, and so on.

- It is really important to wash your screen as soon as possible after you finish printing because you don't want the ink to dry in the screen.

You will need

screen printing kit (page 12)

pencils or textas in multiple colours

set square

ballpoint pen

inks in 5 colours

white cotton T-shirt

scrap paper or card

iron

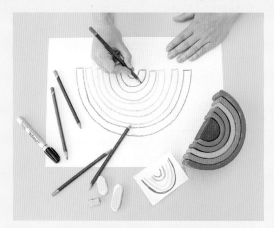

1 Draw your design onto a piece of paper using the same colours you're going to use for printing. We've drawn a rainbow in five colours.

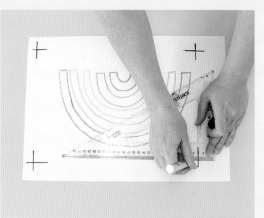

2 Draw a large cross in each corner of your design. These are called registration marks and will be very important in each step of the printing process. Use a set square to make sure they are all straight and aligned with each other.

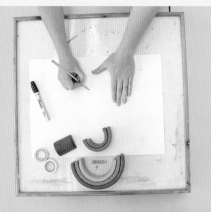

3 Using a light box (or window) and pencil, trace each colour layer onto separate pieces of stencil paper (page 16). You will also need to trace the registration marks (using a pencil) onto EVERY piece of stencil paper – this is very important. Because our rainbow has five colours, we'll need five stencils. Cut out each stencil.

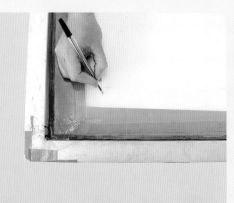

4 Prepare the screen and attach the first stencil (we've started with the smallest blue section) to the front (page 17). Flip the screen over and use a ballpoint pen to draw the registration marks on your screen. The ballpoint pen won't wash out between each print and will indicate where you need to attach each of the five stencils so they are in the same position for each print. Get your squeegee and inks ready.

5 Lay your T-shirt on the work surface and place a piece of scrap paper inside it, so the ink doesn't bleed through to the other side. Place the screen into position over the T-shirt. You will need to place the screen in the same spot for each printed layer, so use your masking tape to mark the four corners of the screen, to use as a positioning guide.

6 Place your screen back inside the tape marks. Spread a generous amount of ink above your design. Start printing with one flood stroke and then apply pressure during your three hard pulls. Carefully lift up the screen from the T-shirt (page 18).

7 Peel off the stencil and wash it, then wash the screen so it's ready for the next print. Make sure the screen is dry before printing your next shape. You will notice that the ballpoint pen registration marks are still on the screen – yay! Dry the first layer using a hair dryer (page 19).

8 Repeat the process for each of the stencils, in different colours, until your design is completed. Heat set the T-shirt with an iron (page 20), and you're ready to wear your new creation!

1 Lay out your fabric. Gather some of your favourite objects and arrange them in a line down the centre of the fabric. Move the objects around until you're happy with their placement. Alternatively, draw some graphic shapes onto paper, cut them out, then arrange them on the fabric. Make a quick sketch of your design, so you remember the positions of the different elements.

2 Trace around each object on a piece of stencil paper. Remember that each shape will need its own piece of stencil paper. Cut the stencils using your scalpel and cutting mat (page 16). Save all the cut-out pieces from each shape – you'll need them in a minute.

3 Attach some doubled-over tape to the back of each cut-out shape and stick them into position on your fabric. This will enable you to register each print.

4 Prepare the screen and attach the first stencil to the front (page 17). Get your squeegee and ink ready. Place the screen over the fabric, carefully lining up the stencil to its corresponding shape on the fabric.

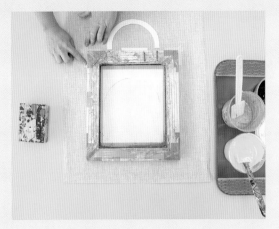

5 Mark the corners of the screen with tape. This will show you where to place your screen. Remove the screen again, then remove the shape from the fabric.

6 Place your screen back inside the tape marks you created – it's in the perfect spot now!

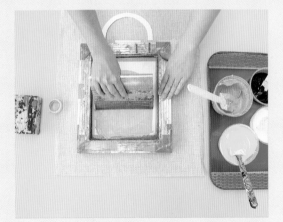

7 Spread a generous amount of ink above your design. Start printing with one flood stroke and then apply pressure during your three hard pulls. Carefully lift up the screen from the fabric (page 18). Peel off the stencil and wash it, then wash and dry the screen. Dry the first print completely using a hair dryer (page 19).

8 Attach the second stencil and use the same process to position and print it. Repeat for each of the stencils. Heat set your finished panel with an iron (page 20).

9 Turn the panel over and fold each edge over 5 mm (¼ in), then press firmly with the iron. Fold over another 5 mm (¼ in) and press again.

10 Pin and then sew around all the edges. Cut off any loose threads.

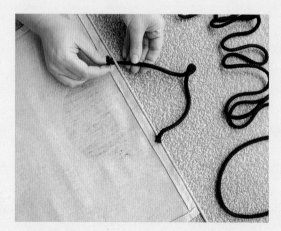

11 Centre the wooden dowel on the top of the panel. Use a needle and thread to neatly sew it to the top of your panel.

12 Thread the cord through the dowel and tie both ends in a knot at the back. Your wall hanging is ready to be hung.

Pillowcase

We each spend A LOT of time in bed doing admin, watching reality TV, cuddling our kiddos and sometimes eating dinner – everything is better in bed! This project is the perfect way to liven up a boring bedroom and it's SO easy! All you need are some plain pillowcases, or you could use this technique to upcycle some old pillowcases in need of a face lift. This project uses a more relaxed version of the registration technique we used for the Wall hanging (page 81).

Handy hints

- If you're printing onto two pillowcases, consider whether you will keep things symmetrical or vary the placement of the print on each pillowcase.
- We suggest using transparent inks here, as they will feel softer against your face.

You will need

coloured paper or cardboard

scissors

ruler

screen printing kit (page 12)

iron

plain pillowcase (we used white)

large piece of scrap paper or card

inks in 3 colours

1 Cut out a selection of shapes from coloured paper – just have fun with it! Pick out your three favourite shapes and place them on a piece of paper, moving the shapes around until you're happy with their placement. This will become your design. You'll need to scale the size up by eye, but that's easy with such simple shapes.

2 Using a pencil, draw the scaled-up version of each shape onto your stencil paper. You will need a different piece of stencil paper for each shape. Cut the stencils using your scalpel and cutting mat (page 16). Save all the cut-out pieces from each shape – you'll need them in a minute.

3 Iron your pillowcase and lay it out on the work surface. Place a large piece of scrap paper inside the pillowcase, so the ink doesn't bleed through to the other side. Arrange the cut-out shapes on the pillowcase. When you're happy with their position, use a doubled-over piece of tape to secure them in place. This will enable you to register each print.

Repeat

pattern printing

Table runner

Sitting around the dinner table with family or friends is one of life's great pleasures, and this project is a beautiful way to personalise this daily ritual. Table runners are such a tactile way to introduce pattern and colour into your home. We love to use ours every day, and you can even make matching napkins if you like, which come in handy during messy mealtimes.

Handy hints

- Choose your motif wisely. Remember that you will have to cut this shape several times, so don't make it too complex.

- The size of the pattern tile you begin with will be the width of your repeat when printing. If you'd prefer to make sure that your last print doesn't run off the edge of your runner, use a screen with a width that divides equally into the length of your runner.

- It can be handy to have a buddy around when printing repeats, to help with drying the prints as you go.

You will need

screen printing kit (page 12)
ruler
iron
linen table runner
tape measure
ink in 1 colour

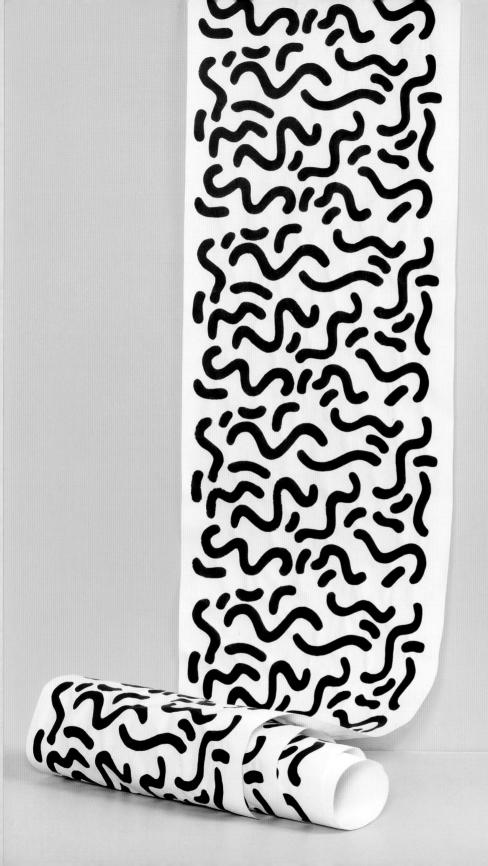

Wallpaper

DIFFICULTY: *Medium*

Cover your walls in your OWN designs with this fun project. If you don't want to commit to a whole wall, then you can just do a long feature panel like the one pictured. You can also use this printing technique to make your own wrapping paper and fabric panels.

Handy hints

• When drying your prints, use the hair dryer on the cool setting so your wallpaper doesn't buckle.

• Wallpaper lining paper is sold at most hardware stores and wallpaper suppliers. The lining paper isn't coated like regular wallpaper, which makes it perfect for printing on.

• The size of the pattern tile you begin with will be the width of your repeat when printing. If you'd prefer to make sure that your last print doesn't run off the edge of your wallpaper, use a screen with a width that divides equally into the length of your wallpaper.

You will need

screen printing kit (page 12)
ruler
paint and paintbrush
tape measure
55 cm (22 in) wide roll of wallpaper lining paper
ink in 1 colour

Elastic-waisted skirt

We've used our printed fabric to create this awesome elastic-waisted skirt. It's a fairly easy project if you're an experienced sewer, but may take a bit more concentration for a first timer. It's so stylish that you'll want to whip one up for every day of the week, PLUS who doesn't love an elastic waistband? Go ahead and have that extra doughnut!

Handy hints

- When deciding on your skirt length, it's better to make it too long (rather than too short), so you can hem it at the end.
- Once you have mastered this project, you can create multiple skirts in all sorts of patterns and lengths.

You will need

screen printing kit (page 12)

long ruler

tape measure

2 m (2 yd) woven fabric (we used 100% cotton poplin)

ink in 1 colour

iron

scissors

pins

sewing machine and thread

about 1 m (1 yd) of 2.5 cm (1 in) wide elastic (exact length will depend on waist measurement)

large safety pin

1 Draw a rectangle onto paper that is slightly smaller than the printable area of your screen. Our rectangle is 28 × 45 cm (11 × 17¾ in). This means that we'll be using 28 cm (11 in) and 45 cm (17¾ in) as the basis for all of our measurements for this project.

2 Fill your rectangle with pattern, making sure that you don't design beyond the boundaries of the rectangle. Using a light box (or window) and pencil, transfer your design onto stencil paper. Carefully cut out the pattern using your scalpel and cutting mat (page 16).

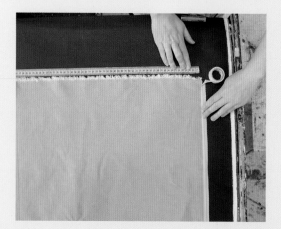

3 Lay a tape measure along the length of your work surface. This will help you determine where to place your screen when printing. Put some doubled-over tape on the back of the tape measure to hold it in position. Line up the edge of your fabric with the edge of the tape measure. Use some tape to hold the fabric in place.

4 Prepare the screen and attach the stencil to the front, making sure that it's straight (page 17). Get your squeegee and ink ready. Place the screen on the fabric, lining up its outer edge to the start of the tape measure – at 0 cm (0 in).

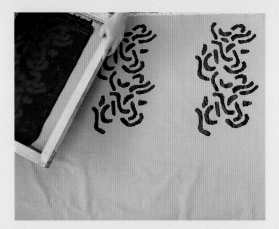

5 Spread a generous amount of ink above your design. Start printing with one flood stroke and then apply pressure during your three hard pulls. Carefully lift up the screen (page 18).

6 Line up the edge of the screen to the 56 cm (22 in) point on the tape measure. Spread a generous amount of ink above your design and print as per step 5. Repeat at 112 cm (44 in), then at 56 cm (22 in) intervals until you reach the end of the fabric. Use a hair dryer to dry your prints as quickly as possible – you don't want the ink to dry in the screen.

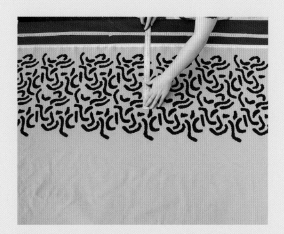

7 Now to fill in the gaps. Line up the edge of the screen to the 28 cm (11 in) point on the tape measure. Spread a generous amount of ink above your design and print as per step 5. Repeat at 84 cm (33 in), then at 56 cm (22 in) intervals until your fabric is full. Use the hair dryer to dry your prints.

8 If you'd like more coverage of print on your fabric (like the skirt pictured on page 102), lift up your tape measure and move your fabric down exactly 45 cm (17¾ in).

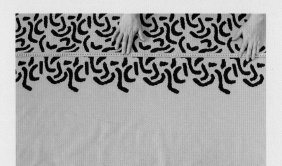

9 Carefully place the tape measure on top of your fabric so that when you place the screen beside it, the edge of the stencil will line up with the edge of the pattern you've already printed. You may need to fiddle around a bit with the placement of the tape measure to get it right.

10 Repeat steps 4–7. When you have finished printing, peel off the stencil and wash it. Wash the screen and squeegee (page 19).

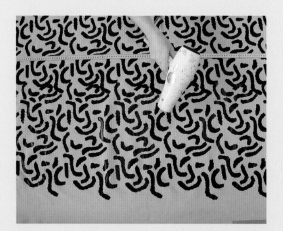

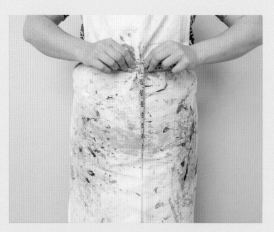

11 Dry your gorgeous new print completely using a hair dryer (page 19). Heat set the fabric with an iron (page 20).

12 Now it's time to sew. Use the tape measure to measure your waist. Take that measurement and double it, then add 2 cm (¾ in) for seam allowance. The model's waist measurement is 80 cm (31½ in), giving a final measurement of 162 cm (63¾ in).

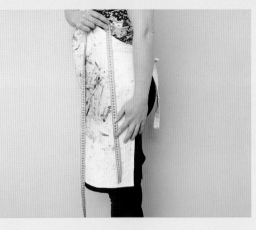

13 Decide on the skirt length you want. Hang the tape measure from your waist, measure to the desired length, then add 8 cm (3 in) to allow for the waistband casing and hem. The model's skirt length is 62 cm (24½ in), giving a final measurement of 70 cm (27½ in).

14 Using a pencil, draw a rectangle on the printed fabric based on your measurements. Ours measures 70 × 162 cm (27½ × 63¾ in). Cut out the rectangle. If you like, you can use the zigzag setting on your sewing machine to sew around the edges to stop them from fraying.

15 To make the casing for the elastic, place the fabric printed side down, fold the top over 1 cm (½ in), then press with an iron.

16 Fold the fabric over 3 cm (1¼ in), so your elastic will fit comfortably through it, and pin in place. Sew along the inside edge of the fold in a straight line, making sure to sew back and forth at each end to secure. Cut off any loose threads.

17 Fold the fabric in half lengthwise with the printed sides together, and pin along the open edge.

18 Sew together, using a 1 cm (½ in) seam allowance, from the bottom of the hem towards the top. Stop sewing when you reach the waistband casing stitch line, as you need to keep this open to feed the elastic through.

19 Get the elastic ready for the waistband. Subtract 2 cm (¾ in) from your waist measurement, then cut a piece of elastic to this measurement. Our model's waist measurement is 80 cm (31½ in) (see step 12), so we've cut a piece of elastic to 78 cm (30¾ in). Attach the safety pin to the end of the elastic and feed it through the casing until it comes out the other end.

20 Make sure the elastic isn't twisted. Sew the two ends of the elastic together and use a straight stitch back and forth to make sure it's secure.

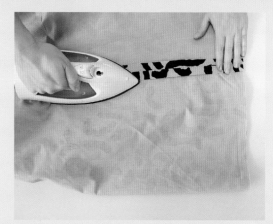

21 Now that the elastic has been put in, you need to go back to the side seam that was left unstitched. Use the sewing machine to continue the stitch line all the way to the top of the waistband, securing the elastic in place.

22 Use the iron to press all the seams open.

23 Try on the skirt while it is still inside out and determine the length. Trim your skirt, remembering that you will lose 2 cm (¾ in) when you hem it. Take the skirt off, then fold the hem up 1 cm (½ in) and press. Fold over another 1 cm (½ in) and press.

24 Use a straight stitch to neatly sew along the inside edge of the hem, approximately 1 cm (½ in) from the finished edge. Turn your skirt right side out and press. It's ready to wear!

Printing on
paper

Art print

DIFFICULTY:
Easy

We love having flowers in the studio at ALL TIMES. Flowers make us happy. This floral paper print is perfect for any flower lover, and printing on paper is an easy, fun and inexpensive way to add some colour to your walls. Better still, it doesn't need water and it blooms all year round!

Handy hints

- When printing onto paper you don't need a flood stroke – just two firm pulls. This is because the ink doesn't sink into paper as it does fabric. If you do too many pulls, your print will bleed and you'll lose that crisp edge.

- Don't dry your prints with a hair dryer, as the paper will warp.

- You don't have to frame your prints for them to look good. Use colourful pins, or string them up on wire with clips to display them in your home.

- Mix up your look by printing on different coloured paper; black is a bold choice.

- A cluster of prints in various sizes always looks great.

You will need

screen printing kit (page 12)
paper printing inks in 2 colours
heavy-weight paper in various colours
ready-to-hang frame (optional)

1 Draw your design onto paper. We've gone with a bold floral design here, although you might be inspired by the graphic wedge of cheese we've included in the main photo, just for fun. For inspiration, collect flowers from your garden or look through magazines or photos. Transfer your design onto stencil paper, then cut your stencils (page 16). This design has two colours, so you will need two stencils. Prepare the screen and attach the first stencil (the petals) to the front (page 17). Get your squeegee and inks ready.

2 Lay your paper on the work surface and place the screen on top. Spread a generous amount of ink above your design and carefully print your first layer (page 18). Remember, because you're printing on paper, you only need two firm pulls – and you don't need a flood stroke. We suggest doing a few extra prints, so if you mess one up you have backups.

3 You MUST let the first layer air-dry before adding the next one. While you're waiting for the print to dry, peel off the stencil and wash it, then wash and dry the screen (page 19). Attach your second stencil (the circle) to the screen.

4 Once your first layer is dry, print the second stencil in the second colour using two firm pulls. Make sure your print is COMPLETELY dry, then hang it on the wall. Frame it if you like.

Wrapping paper

Wrapping presents is so much fun, especially with your own custom wrapping paper. We first used this technique for printing wrapping paper at a holiday market many years ago and it was a huge hit! It's a good idea to make it in big batches, so you'll always have some on hand. Plus it sounds really impressive when you casually mention that YOU printed it!

Handy hints

- Don't dry your print with a hair dryer, as the paper will warp.
- We've used opaque white ink on blue paper here, but white ink on brown paper looks awesome, too.
- When printing, remember to use only one or two pulls. If you do too many, your paper will warp.
- We prefer to print onto matte paper. Glossy paper can be slippery and doesn't absorb the ink as well.

You will need

screen printing kit (page 12)
ruler
tape measure
2 m (2 yd) roll of paper (matte finish) in your choice of colour
paper printing ink in 1 colour

1 Draw up some ideas for your design. We've chosen a flower and some graphic shapes in a 20 cm (8 in) wide repeat tile. The depth of your tile will depend on the size of your screen – ours is 30 cm (12 in) deep.

2 Transfer your design onto stencil paper, then cut your stencil (page 16).

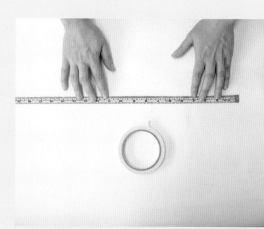

3 Lay out your tape measure along the edge of your work surface. Put some doubled-over tape on the back of the tape measure to hold the tape in position. Roll out your paper along the length of the tape measure. Tape down the corners of the paper to keep it in place. You will be printing at 20 cm (8 in) intervals.

4 Prepare the screen and attach the stencil to the front, making sure it's straight and centred (page 17). Get your squeegee and ink ready.

5 Place the screen on the paper, lining up its outer edge with 0 cm (0 in) on the tape measure. Spread a generous amount of ink above your design and print using two firm pulls – you don't need a flood stroke because ink doesn't sink into paper as it does fabric. Carefully lift up the screen (page 18).

6 Repeat this process at 40 cm (16 in), 80 cm (32 in) and 120 cm (48 in), and continue at 40 cm (16 in) intervals until you reach the end of the paper. Then allow the prints to air-dry completely. Because air-drying takes some time, you need to peel off the stencil and wash it, then wash the screen so the ink doesn't dry in the mesh (page 19).

7 Make sure the screen is dry, then reattach your stencil. Line up the screen to the 20 cm (8 in) point on the tape measure. Spread a generous amount of ink above your design and print as per step 5.

8 Repeat at the 60 cm (24 in) point, then continue at 40 cm (16 in) intervals until your paper is full. Allow your gorgeous new wrapping paper to air-dry and then get wrapping!

Greeting card

Some of our most treasured possessions are the handmade greeting cards we've hoarded over the years. Greeting cards are the perfect little canvas to design for. And because you're printing onto cardboard, it's also an opportunity to experiment with patterns and colours without committing them to fabric. This technique also works with gift tags and gift boxes (see opposite and page 126), or you could even print your own postcards. The flower design we've used shows how it's often the more basic shapes that look the most striking when printed.

Handy hints

- The instructions for this project are for the white flower greeting cards, although we've included a simple graphic rose card in the photograph opposite as well.

- Make a bunch of cards at the same time so you never get caught without one.

- You can make cards in whatever size or shape you want.

- A smaller screen definitely makes this project a little easier.

- Remember, don't use a hair dryer to dry the prints, even if you're tempted! The heat will warp the card.

You will need

screen printing kit (page 12)
ruler
coloured cardboard
scissors
bone folder (or use a scalpel)
paper printing inks in 2 colours

1 Draw a rectangle measuring 15 × 30 cm (6 × 12 in) onto your cardboard, then cut it out. Fold the cardboard in half, using a bone folder to create a crisp fold. Alternatively, lightly score down the middle of the cardboard using a metal ruler and scalpel, then fold the card in half along the score line. Unfold the cardboard and lay it flat on the table.

2 Draw your design. We've gone with a simple flower design: the white petals make the first stencil, and the yellow circle is the second stencil. Transfer your design onto stencil paper, then cut your stencils (page 16).

3 Prepare the screen and attach the first stencil (the petals) to the front (page 17). Get your squeegee and inks ready.

4 Position the screen over the right-hand side of the cardboard (when folded, this will be the front of your card).

5 Spread a generous amount of ink above your design. Print the first layer using two firm pulls – you don't need a flood stroke (page 18). This is because the ink doesn't sink into the cardboard as it does on fabric.

6 Remove the screen and allow your print to air-dry. Don't use the hair dryer, as it will warp the card. Because air-drying takes some time, you need to peel off the stencil and wash it, then wash the screen so the ink doesn't dry in the mesh (page 19).

7 Attach the second stencil (the circle) to the screen. Place the screen on top of your card so that the circle sits in the middle of the flower petals. Print the second layer as per step 5.

8 Remove the screen and allow your print to air-dry – don't use the hair dryer. Wash the stencil and screen. Once your print is completely dry, you can re-fold the card in half.

Gift box

Ooh-la-la! These boxes make even the most ordinary gift seem SUPER fancy! They are also great for storing all your knick-knacks, and look so cute all stacked up. For this project we've designed a random geometric floral. To see the finished product, turn to page 122.

You will need

screen printing kit (page 12)
flat-packed cardboard gift boxes
(matte finish)
paper printing ink in 1 colour
scrap paper

Handy hints

- You can buy flat-packed gift boxes from stationery stores, or try online if you're having trouble sourcing them.

- Buy the boxes with a matte finish – most printing inks don't love a high-gloss surface.

1 Draw your design onto paper. We've drawn a simple floral pattern that will cover the whole box.

2 Transfer your design onto stencil paper, making sure that the stencil is slightly larger than the flat box. Cut your stencil (page 16).

3 Prepare the screen and attach the stencil to the front (page 17). Get your squeegee and ink ready.

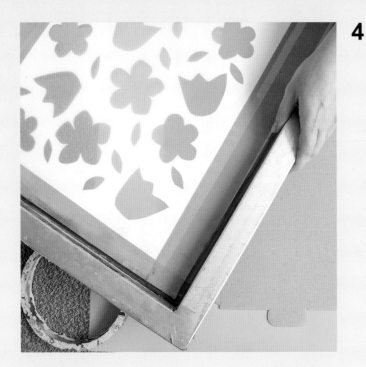

4 Lay your box out flat on the work surface, with some scrap paper underneath. Lay the screen on top of the flat box, making sure that the pattern covers the entire box.

5 Spread a generous amount of ink above your design. Use two firm pulls to print your design – you don't need a flood stroke (page 18). Be mindful that when you print over the edges of the box the ink will gather in those spots, so try to avoid using too much pressure when printing.

6 Remove the screen – the box may stick to the screen, so be careful. Wash the stencil and screen (page 19).

7 Allow your print to air-dry completely – don't use the hair dryer. Assemble your beautiful box.

Printing on
wood

These patterns and shapes make us so happy (and hungry)! In this chapter we're inspired by
Scandi food illustrations, Memphis-style patterns and some of our favourite colours.

Into the woods

Printing on wood is REALLY fun. It's a lot like printing on paper – you don't need a flood stroke and you only need a couple of firm pulls with the squeegee.

You can make so many things with wood. We show you how to make a plywood art panel for your wall and a super practical (and super cute) wooden planter box. The other great thing about printing on wood is there's NO HEAT SETTING – yay! You may get the odd splinter, but it's totally worth it. Let's take your printing to the next level with these fun plywood projects.

Wall panel

Printing onto a piece of plywood is a great way to create an instant piece of artwork for your home – and it doesn't need to be framed. If you like, make a bunch of them and group them together (that always looks impressive). For this project we were inspired by one of our favourite activities – eating!

Handy hints

- To achieve a crisp print use an opaque ink, as transparent ink is not as thick and can bleed.
- Check out the offcuts bin at your local hardware store. You may find a piece that's perfect for your wall panel.
- No need to just stick to squares and rectangles – cut your plywood into any shape you like.
- We attached small D-rings and wire for hanging. You can find them in your local hardware or art store.

You will need

fine sandpaper
30 × 30 cm (12 × 12 in) piece of plywood
damp cloth
screen printing kit (page 12)
inks in 2 colours
D-rings and small picture screws
screwdriver
hanging wire

1 Sand the edges of your plywood panel. Wipe off the dust with a slightly damp cloth.

2 Draw your design onto paper. For this project, we decided on a juicy pear. This design has two colours, one for the pear and one for the stem, so you will need to cut two stencils. Alternatively, be inspired by one of the other designs shown in the photo on page 134.

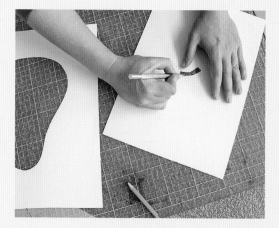

3 Transfer the design onto stencil paper, then cut the stencils using your scalpel and cutting mat (page 16). Prepare the screen and attach the first stencil (the pear shape) to the front (page 17). Get your squeegee and inks ready. Lay the wood panel on the work surface.

4 Place the screen on the wood panel. Spread a generous amount of ink above your design. Steady your screen with one hand and give the squeegee two hard pulls across the screen (page 18). Remember, you don't need a flood stroke when printing onto wood.

5 Carefully lift up the screen. Peel off the stencil and wash it, then wash and dry the screen. Dry this layer using a hair dryer before printing the next stencil (page 19).

6 Attach the second stencil (the stem) to the screen and place it on the wood panel, positioning the screen so the stem stencil is sitting on top of the pear. Following step 4, apply the ink and use your squeegee to give two hard pulls.

7 Wash the stencil and screen. Admire your new plywood panel! Make sure your print is dry.

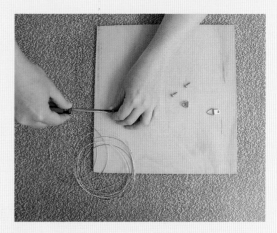

8 Attach D-rings to the back of the panel using small screws. Thread the hanging wire between the D-rings. Secure at each end. Find the perfect spot on your wall to hang your panel!

Planter box

Okay, now THIS is a project that will impress your buddies. It's not that hard to make. We promise! And once you make one you'll be addicted. These boxes make perfect planters, but we also use them in different sizes for clutter, toys, books, pets … They're great for organising a child's (or adult's) room; print different faces or patterns on each box, so they start to remember which box contains what.

Handy hints

- For this project you will need a large piece of plywood. Use a jigsaw or handsaw to cut the plywood yourself, or ask the staff at the hardware store to cut it for you, into five pieces, as specified at right (there will be a few little offcuts). Mark your panels in pencil as A, B, C, D and E.

- To make smaller or larger boxes, simply adjust the measurements given in the materials list. The measurements given here are to make one medium box (the blue box shown opposite).

- Use some scrap offcuts of plywood to test your colours.

You will need

screen printing kit (page 12)

30 × 150 cm (11¾ × 60 in) piece of 17 mm (¾ in) plywood, cut into: three panels (A, B and C), 30 × 30 cm (11¾ × 11¾ in); two panels (D and E), 26.6 cm × 30 cm (10½ × 11¾ in)

fine sandpaper

damp cloth

opaque ink in 1 colour

quick-dry wood glue or PVA

electric drill

8 × 12 mm (½ in) screws

Printing on
corkboard

Trivets and coasters

DIFFICULTY:
Easy

Trivets and coasters are criminally under-appreciated. Every time we see the burnt ring on the studio kitchen table we curse ourselves for not embracing them earlier. We love these printed coasters for the kitchen, coffee table or even under potted plants. You can buy blank cork products at most dollar stores – they usually come in a multi-pack so you can really go wild with different patterns and colours. For this project we've used our favourite leopard print design in crisp white.

Handy hints

- These projects work best with opaque ink.
  - To extend the life of your printed cork products, seal them with a light coat of varnish. It's a good idea to test your varnish on a spare printed coaster before committing to the final pieces.
- You can use the same technique to print a series of cork placemats.

You will need
screen printing kit (page 12)
a selection of cork trivets or coasters
ink in 1 colour
varnish (optional)

1 Draw a pattern of your choice – we can't resist a leopard print. Place your cork trivet or coaster on the sheet of stencil paper and trace around it. Then, use a light box (or window) to transfer the design onto the stencil paper or draw it freehand (page 16), filling in the outline with your pattern.

2 Place the stencil paper on the cutting mat and use your scalpel to carefully cut out the design.

3 Prepare the screen and attach the stencil to the front (page 17). Get your squeegee and ink ready.

4 Place the screen on top of the trivet, taking care to centre the design.

5 Spread a generous amount of ink above your design, steady the screen with one hand and then give the squeegee two hard pulls across the screen (page 18). You don't need a flood stroke when printing onto cork. Carefully remove the screen.

6 If you're printing multiple trivets (or coasters), repeat steps 4–5 until you have printed all of your items. Admire your gorgeous new trivets. Peel off the stencil and wash it, then wash the screen (page 19). Before use, allow the ink to dry for 1 hour, and for at least 24 hours if you're going to varnish them (see Handy hints).

Cork pinboard

Organise your life with this dreamy pinboard that doubles as a work of art. We found this large corkboard at a dollar store – they come in a large range of shapes and sizes. Think of the board as a huge blank canvas where you can create any look you want – keep it simple with just a few scattered shapes or fill your board with colour. Whatever you decide, we're pretty sure your new pinboard will turn you into the organised person you always knew you could be!

Handy hints

- It can be tricky to print right to the edge if your corkboard has a frame, so try to focus your design on the middle of the board.
- Using opaque ink will really make the colours pop on the brown cork. If you use transparent ink, then some of the brown colour will still be visible under your prints.

You will need

screen printing kit (page 12)
inks in 4 or 5 colours
cork pinboard
a selection of push-pins

1 Draw your design onto paper. We've gone for a mix of animal eyes and a simple floral design.

2 Transfer your designs onto stencil paper, then cut your stencils (page 16). You will need two stencils for the eyes, and one stencil for the flowers.

3 Prepare the screen and attach the first stencil to the front (page 17). Get your squeegee and inks ready. Lay your pinboard on the work surface, then place the screen within the frame of the board. Spread a generous amount of ink above your design, steady the screen with one hand and then give the squeegee two hard pulls across the screen (page 18). You don't need a flood stroke when printing onto cork.

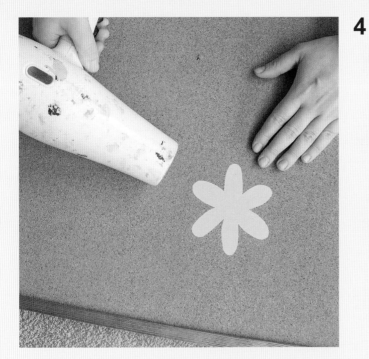

4 Carefully lift up the screen from the pinboard. Use a hair dryer to dry the first print, so you don't smudge it when you move the screen to the next spot. If you like, repeat the process a few more times (in the same colour) on other areas of the board. Peel off the stencil and wash it, then wash and dry your screen so it's ready for the next print (page 19).

5 Prepare your next stencil. Repeat steps 3–4 until the pinboard is filled with as many prints as you like. We love to use four or five colours, but you can stick to one or two if you prefer. Allow the pinboard to dry for 24 hours, then hang it up and start pinning!

Printing using
metallic foil

The Golden Girls have arrived! Our obsession with Ancient Egypt and Memphis patterns has inspired the designs in this chapter.

Solid gold

We've always had a love affair with gold foil. There are many types of metallic foils out there but, let's face it, gold will always be number one in our hearts. The process of foil printing has a few more steps than regular printing, but it is totally worth the extra effort.

What you're actually printing is the glue. Foil printing glue is a thick, stinky substance – you use the glue in the same way that you'd use ink in regular screen printing. The foil, available in art and craft stores, comes in a sheet or on a roll – it's a very thin layer of foil with a plastic backing. Once you've printed the glue, you'll need to make sure it's completely dry and then lay the foil over the top. ALWAYS ensure that you lay the foil gold-side UP. This next part takes some practice, but you'll need to apply pressure and heat to the foil so that it adheres to the glue. The technique that has worked for us is using a bone folder (these are a total lifesaver) to apply smooth, long strokes across the foil and then using an iron to apply heat. We repeat this process of applying pressure and then heat a total of four times, and then allow it to cool completely before removing the plastic layer.

We've always dreamed of visiting Egypt – preferably in a time machine so we can swap eyeliner tips with Cleopatra – so the projects in this chapter are inspired by these daydreams.

Clutch bag

We love this simple clutch; it's big enough to fit the essentials, and the shimmering gold adds some glam to your outfit. This print was inspired by all the gold treasure and jewels that were found in Tutankhamen's tomb. We've kept the shapes very organic, but any simple, graphic shapes would work really well.

Handy hints

- A bone folder is usually used for folding paper or card, but it's also handy for applying metallic foil to fabric. It's a good tool to have in your craft box.
- You can zigzag stitch around your inside seams for extra durability.

You will need

screen printing kit (page 12)

iron

50 × 90 cm (20 × 35 in) 100% cotton (pre-washed)

foil glue for fabric

gold foil for fabric

scissors

bone folder or pencil

tailor's chalk

tape measure

28 cm (11 in) zipper

pins

sewing machine (with zipper foot) and thread

1 Draw your design onto paper, transfer it onto stencil paper, then cut your stencil (page 16).

2 Iron your fabric and lay it flat on the work surface, right side up. We've chosen to print the two panels on a large piece of fabric and then cut it after it has been printed. Prepare the screen and attach the stencil to the front (page 17).

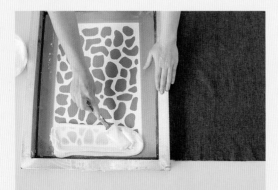

3 For printing, we will be using foil glue instead of ink. Place the screen on one edge of the fabric (this will be your first panel). Using a spatula, spread a generous amount of glue above your design.

4 Start printing with one flood stroke followed by four hard pulls (page 18). Foil glue is a little thicker than regular screen printing ink, which is why you need to use a few more pulls.

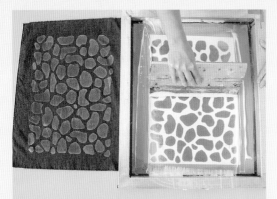

5 Carefully lift up your screen and repeat steps 3–4 on your second panel. Peel off the stencil and wash it, then wash your screen (page 19). Allow the glue to dry completely – use a hair dryer to speed up the process.

6 Cut a piece of foil slightly bigger than your design, to ensure the glued areas are completely covered. Carefully place the foil on top of the printed glue, making sure the foil is gold-side up. Smooth it out with your hands and press down hard using long, smooth strokes (you can also use a bone folder or pencil for this).

7 With the iron set on hot, iron over the top of the gold foil, pressing firmly down with the iron. Make sure you iron over all the areas that have glue printed on them. Repeat this process four times in total: apply long, smooth strokes over the gold foil (step 6), iron firmly, let it cool, then repeat. This will ensure your foil is applied evenly.

8 Allow the foil to cool completely, then carefully peel back the foil. It's VERY important that the foil has cooled before you peel it off; if it's still warm, the glue will be sticky and your foil won't have set properly.

9 Lay out the printed fabric and use tailor's chalk to draw two rectangles: 32 × 44 cm (12½ × 17 in) – rectangle A; and 32 × 22 cm (12½ × 8½ in) – rectangle B. Cut out the two rectangles. Place your zipper face down along the 32 cm (12½ in) length of rectangle A, making sure the foiled side is facing up. Pin into place.

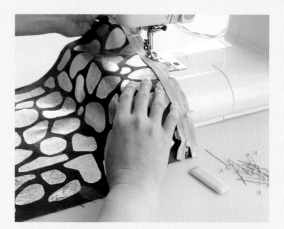

10 Put the zipper foot on your sewing machine. With the zipper head facing towards you, sew along the edge of the zipper until you reach the halfway point.

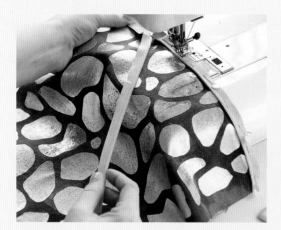

11 Open your zipper completely, as the foot cannot go over the zipper head. Continue sewing until you reach the end of the zipper and then sew back and forth to secure the line of stitching. Remove the pins.

12 Line up the unsewn side of the zipper along the 32 cm (12½ in) side of rectangle B. Make sure that the zipper is facing down and the foiled side of rectangle B is facing up – the foiled sides of both rectangles should be facing each other. Pin the zipper to the edge of rectangle B.

13 Sew along the edge of the zipper until you reach the halfway point and then open the zipper completely, as the foot cannot go over the zipper head. Continue to sew until you reach the end of the fabric.

14 Close the zipper halfway. Your zipper is in! Use an iron to press open the zipper seams.

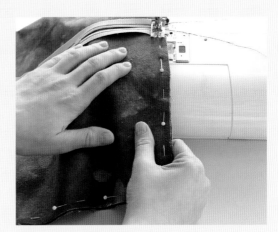

15 Fold your fabric over with the right sides facing each other and pin around the base and sides, making sure that the zipper ends are matched up. The zipper will be hidden under the fold of the finished clutch, so don't worry if it looks a bit strange at this stage – it will all work out!

16 Remove the zipper foot from the sewing machine and attach the straight stitch foot. Using a 1 cm (½ in) seam allowance, sew around the sides and base of the clutch. Trim the edges and cut off any loose threads. Turn right way out and push out the corners. Press with a cool iron, fold in half and your clutch is ready to use.

Santa sack

DIFFICULTY:
Hard

What's not to love about this chic Santa sack? It adds a touch of glam to the festive season and then does double duty as a small laundry bag or library bag during the non-festive months. We went with super simple circles for our print, but any large, bold shape would work well. To make the sack, we used some indigo dyed fabric that we found in our stash. We love the way the gold foil and deep indigo look together – it's a match made in heaven!

Handy hint

- Instead of the circular design we've used here, you could print some festive motifs on your Santa sack, such as stars, snowflakes or Christmas trees.

You will need

screen printing kit (page 12)

scissors

iron

90 × 110 cm (35 × 43 in) piece of cotton fabric in your choice of colour (pre-washed)

foil glue for fabric

gold foil for fabric

bone folder or pencil

pinking shears (optional)

sewing machine and thread

pins

stitch unpicker

large safety pin

120 cm (47 in) cotton rope or cord

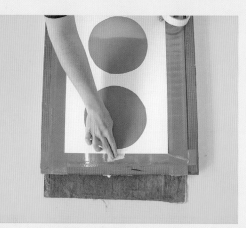

1 Draw your design onto paper, transfer it onto stencil paper, then cut your stencil (page 16). Our design was inspired by ancient gold coins.

2 Cut your fabric into two 44 × 52 cm (17 × 20½ in) pieces. Iron the fabric and lay it flat on the work surface. Prepare the screen and attach the stencil to the front (page 17).

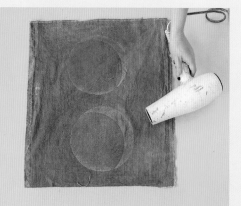

3 For printing, we will be using foil glue instead of ink. Place the screen on top of the fabric. Spread a generous amount of glue above your design. Start printing with one flood stroke followed by four hard pulls (page 18). Foil glue is a little thicker than regular screen printing ink, which is why you need to use a few more pulls.

4 Carefully lift up the screen and repeat step 3 on your second piece of fabric. Peel off the stencil and wash it, then wash your screen (page 19). Allow the glue to dry completely – use a hair dryer to speed up the process.

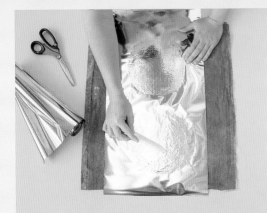

5 Cut a piece of foil slightly bigger than your design, to ensure the glued areas are completely covered. Carefully place the foil on top of the printed glue, making sure the foil is gold-side up. Smooth it out with your hands and press down hard using long, smooth strokes (you can also use a bone folder or pencil for this).

6 With the iron set on hot, iron over the top of the gold foil, pressing firmly down with the iron. Make sure you iron over all the areas that have glue printed there. Repeat this process four times in total: apply long, smooth strokes over the gold foil (step 5), iron firmly, let it cool, then repeat. This will ensure your foil is applied evenly.

7 Allow the foil to cool completely, then carefully peel back the foil. It's VERY important that the foil has cooled before you peel it off; if it's still warm, the glue will be sticky and your foil won't have set properly.

8 Using pinking shears, cut around the edges of the fabric to create two rectangles measuring 42 × 50 cm (16½ × 20 in). Alternatively, sew a zigzag stitch around the edges to prevent them from fraying.

9 To create a neat hem, place a piece of fabric right (foiled) side down and fold the top 42 cm (16½ in) edge over 5 mm (¼ in). Press. Fold over again and press, then sew along the fold. Repeat for the other piece. This will be the opening of the sack.

10 Place the two pieces of fabric right (foiled) sides together, and pin the three unhemmed sides. Sew down these three sides, leaving the opening of the sack unsewn.

11 Press open the side seams.

12 Now to the unsewn side – your opening. Fold the fabric back towards you around the full perimeter of the opening so that you have 1 cm (½ in) of fabric above your stitch line. Pin.

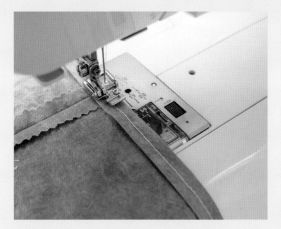

13 Sew around the perimeter of the sack opening, using the existing stitch line as a guide.

14 Flip the Santa sack so the sewn seams are on the inside and the gold foil is facing out. Use a stitch unpicker to open up one of the side seams at the top of your sack. Unpick 2 cm (¾ in) only.

15 Attach a large safety pin to one end of the cotton rope. Thread the rope through the opening in the side seam and feed the rope through the casing around the top of the sack, using your safety pin to help guide it through.

16 Pull lightly on the rope. Knot the ends of the rope together and you're done!

Printing without
a screen

Sometimes you need to break the rules.
Ditch the screen and let loose with the projects in this chapter.

Fresh prints

We are sometimes asked if it's possible to print onto fabric without using a screen. The answer is YES. There are days when you may not feel like cleaning out screens, and these easy techniques show you how to create incredible fabric designs without needing to get out your screen at all. It's also a great, tactile way of printing that's perfect for kids.

Fabric planter

DIFFICULTY:
Medium

We love masking tape! We use it every day to attach stencils to our screens, but in this project we've used it instead of a stencil. Here the tape is used to create a random pattern, but you can create stripes, checks or any kind of shape. These containers are made using heavy canvas, so they hold their shape well. They work well as planters, but they're also perfect for organising your life.

Handy hints

- Use a good-quality masking tape, so it adheres to the fabric properly.
- You can cut shapes out of masking tape to make spots or squiggles – any shape you like.
- These containers look great in a group and you can adjust the pattern for any size.

You will need

iron

70 cm (28 in) heavy-weight fabric (we used canvas)

masking tape (in any width)

foam roller and painting tray

ink in 1 colour

hair dryer

tape measure

pencil

set square (optional)

scissors

pins

sewing machine and thread

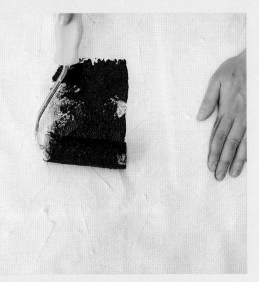

1 Iron your fabric and lay it flat on the work surface. Use masking tape to attach each corner of the fabric to the table to secure it in place. Tear off strips of masking tape and apply them randomly to the fabric to create a pattern.

2 Load up your foam roller with ink and very carefully begin rolling the ink over your taped fabric. Try to not let the tape flick up.

3 Slowly make your way across the fabric with the roller, covering it in an even layer of ink – you don't want any thicker areas of ink or it will take too long to dry. Use a hair dryer to make sure your whole design is completely dry.

4 Now comes the fun part! Carefully peel off all the pieces of tape to reveal your design.

5 Iron your fabric to heat set it (page 20) and then lay it out. Cut one rectangle measuring 46 × 62 cm (18 × 24½ in). If you like, use a set square to ensure your rectangle is straight.

6 With the remaining fabric, cut two circles each with a diameter of 19.5 cm (7¾ in).

7 Fold the rectangular piece of fabric in half, with the longest sides together and right (printed) sides facing each other, and pin along the long side. Sew along this side, leaving a 10 cm (4 in) gap at the end, so you can turn the fabric right way out when you're finished.

8 Open up one end of your sewn tube and lay one of the fabric circles on top of the opening, with the right side facing down. Pin the perimeter of the circle to the edge of the tube. Sew around the perimeter.

9 Repeat step 8 for the other end of the tube.

10 Turn right side out through the unsewn gap, then pin along the open gap. Carefully sew up the gap, making sure to sew back and forth at each end to secure.

11 Now push the top of the tube inside itself so both circles are touching each other.

12 Fold the fabric over at the top and you're done!

Square scarf

This hand-printed scarf is so easy and satisfying to make. For this project, you'll be combining stencil cutting with hand painting. We recommend choosing bold and painterly designs to really embrace everything that is awesome about this technique.

Handy hints

- Use a natural fibre such as cotton, linen or a heavy silk for your scarf.
- Embrace rough brushstrokes, to give your design different tones of colour.
- It is best to use a flat, wide watercolour brush for this technique, as this holds a lot of ink and has smooth bristles.

You will need

medium-size flat, smooth paintbrush

paint

drawing paper

light box or window

pencil

stencil paper

scalpel

cutting mat

140 × 140 cm (55 × 55 in) pre-sewn scarf made from a natural fibre

ink in 1 colour

hair dryer

iron

1 Paint your design onto a piece of paper the same size as your stencil paper. We've used bold painterly strokes to create our design.

2 Using a light box (or window) and pencil, transfer your design onto stencil paper. Carefully cut out the pattern using your scalpel and cutting mat (page 16).

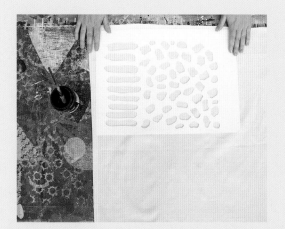

3 Lay the scarf out flat on the work surface, right side up. Place the stencil on the bottom corner of the scarf. Gather your flat paintbrush and ink.

4 Paint over the top of the stencil using flat brushstrokes until the entire stencil is filled with ink. Don't worry if the brushstrokes are a bit uneven, as this gives you lovely tones in your colour.

5 Carefully lift the stencil off your scarf and set the stencil aside to dry.

6 Dry your painted design using a hair dryer (page 19). Note that because the ink is often thicker in some sections when using this technique, it may take longer to dry than a traditional screen print.

7 Once your stencil is dry, place it on the other corner of your scarf. Repeat step 4.

8 Repeat this process of painting and drying until the whole scarf is filled. Make sure your entire scarf is dried using a hair dryer. Heat set the fabric with an iron (page 20) and your scarf is ready to wear!

Melting ice cream backpack

DIFFICULTY:
Hard

Many years ago we coined the term, 'Melting ice cream printing' to describe this crazy technique – and I'm sure you can see why! This method of printing has been a popular one in our workshops because it's so easy and the results are always amazing. This easy backpack pattern is perfect for day-to-day use. We use ours as a day pack when we are travelling – it's comfy to wear and folds up to almost nothing – PLUS it always guarantees lots of compliments! We went with bright and pastel colours here, but you can use any colour palette you like.

Handy hints

- Think about your colour palette. We love to mix brights and pastels, as they always work so well together.
- This is gonna get MESSY, so think about putting down a drop cloth and have a container ready to scoop up the excess ink.
- Make sure you apply a good amount of pressure when you pull your ink, otherwise there will be too much ink left on the fabric, which makes drying it a little tricky.

You will need

drop cloth or plastic tablecloth

iron

1 m (1 yd) fabric (we used a heavy-weight cotton drill)

masking tape

a few spoons or spatulas

inks in 5–7 colours

squeegee

rag

empty containers for excess ink

hair dryer

tape measure

pencil

scissors

set square (optional)

iron

pins

sewing machine and thread

1.5 m (1.5 yd) narrow cord, cut in half

large safety pin

1 Cover your table with the drop cloth or plastic tablecloth to protect it. Iron your fabric and lay it out on the table, right side up. Use masking tape to attach each corner of the fabric to the table to secure it in place. Use the spoon or spatula to dollop generous blobs of ink ALL over your fabric. Don't worry about keeping it uniform; you want a random and crazy mix of blobs.

2 Once you have a good amount of random blobs over the fabric, position your squeegee at the top of your fabric on a 45-degree angle. Use the squeegee to pull the ink from the top of the fabric to the bottom. Do this very slowly. This will smudge all the colours together to give you that signature 'melting ice cream' look. Clean off your squeegee with a rag between each pull.

3 Repeat this step until all of your blobs have been 'printed' (smudged!). You've made a bit of a mess, haven't you? Use a spatula to scoop the excess ink into an empty container. Wash the squeegee and clean all the ink off yourself. Congratulations if you're not covered in ink!

4 Use a hair dryer to make sure the printed fabric is completely dry. This could take some time depending on how thick the ink is.

5 Once the fabric is dry, cut out two rectangles measuring 45 × 50 cm (18 × 20 in). If you like, use a set square to ensure your rectangles are straight. Heat set each piece with an iron (page 20).

6 Place both rectangles together with the right sides facing each other. Pin along the two long sides.

7 Mark your fabric 3 cm (1¼ in) from the top and bottom, on both pinned sides. This will let you know where to start and stop sewing.

8 Sew along each side, remembering to start and stop 3 cm (1¼ in) from the top and bottom.

9 Using an iron, press the side seams open. Fold over the top edge 1.5 cm (½ in) and press with the iron.

10 Sew around the perimeter of the folded edge.

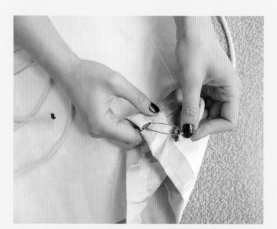

11 Take your first piece of cord and attach the safety pin to one end of the cord. Thread the cord through the right side opening, then through the whole perimeter of the tube so the cord end comes out the right side.

12 Take your second piece of cord and thread it through the left side opening, then through the whole perimeter of the tube so the cord end comes out the left side.

13 Tightly pull the cords on each side. These are going to be your backpack straps.

14 Feed the right side cord pieces through the neck of the backpack and tuck them into the 3 cm (1¼ in) gap you left for them at the bottom of the backpack. Pin into place. Repeat this step for the left side cord pieces.

15 Sew the cords into place and sew up the bottom seam of the backpack.

16 Turn inside out, press with the iron and your backpack is ready to try on.

Thank you

We'd like to give a special THANK YOU to the amazing Rachel Wood, whose tireless enthusiasm and talent always amazes us. Thank you for your humour, creativity and endless patience – you mean the world to us. We love you.

We'd also like to thank the following individuals and organisations for their support, wisdom, inspiration and laughs during the making of this book: Martin Reftel and Jess Reftel Evans, Loran McDougall, Jessica Lowe, Wayne and Jan Gardner, Kerry and Brian Davies, Jude Wright, Deborah Maxwell, Andrew Lonie, Anna Davies, Sarah Davies, Gemma Patford, David Stewart at Permaset, Kip & Co, Melbourne Artists' Supplies, Beci Orpin, Hardie Grant, Wunder Weave and all our wonderful students. Big thanks to Emma Cutri, Laura Johnston and Popcorn Maxwell for your awesome modelling skills!

Finally, we'd like to thank YOU. Thank you for picking up this book. We are so excited to have you as the newest member of our screen-printing cult!

Happy printing!

xxx Jess and Lara

From Jess

THANK YOU to the two loves of my life – Nick and Milo Maxwell. To my INCREDIBLE Mama, I love you. Thank you to Debba and Panda for always being my loving cheerleaders. To the real writer in the family, Bonnie McBride – I'm so, so proud of you. Thank you to my beautiful family for their love and support – Nini and Keith Elliott, Alex Maxwell, Samii Kilian, Kate and Sarah Lonie. To one of my favourite people on earth, Lucas Grogan, thank you for all the quality chats. To my QUEENS, Claire Davies and Hannah Ward – you're the best friends a gal could ask for. And finally, my girl Lara Davies. My partner-in-crime. Your strength and creativity impress me every day – I can't wait to see what adventures await us!

From Lara

Thank you to my two darling boys, Frankie and Max. I love you to bits! Thank you to my family, Kerry, Brian, Anna and Sarah Davies, and Massimo, Jackson and Ellie De Paola, for your ongoing love and support. Thank you to Teo, Jan, Wayne and Gina Gardner for your constant support, love and encouragement. Thank you to these gorgeous friends, who are always there cheering for me: Nick and Lara Huggins, Nina Whitton, Kaya Clifford, Jessica Scott, Heidi Wiebke, Beck Wallman and Ben Lumb, Dan Peterson, Gaby Piemonte and Bianca Valentine. Thank you to my friends by the sea: Jade Ogilvie, Kate Heppel, Norna Boyd, Emily Limb, Lou Garland and Skye Patel, Sam Barry, Linden McCormack and Fay Agterhuis, for your kindness and support while I was writing this book. Thank you to the GROW family and Karen Hermann for being so kind and always asking me, 'How is the book going?'! Lastly, thank you to Jessie for constantly inspiring me and making me laugh every single day we work together!

Published in 2018 by Hardie Grant Books, an imprint of Hardie Grant Publishing

Hardie Grant Books (Melbourne)
Building 1, 658 Church Street
Richmond, Victoria 3121

Hardie Grant Books (London)
5th & 6th Floors
52–54 Southwark Street
London SE1 1UN

hardiegrantbooks.com

A Cataloguing-in-Publication entry is available from the catalogue of
the National Library of Australia at www.nla.gov.au

Print Play
ISBN 978 1 74379 340 4

10 9 8 7 6 5 4 3 2 1

Publisher: Melissa Kayser
Managing Editor: Marg Bowman
Project Editor: Loran McDougall
Editor: Kim Rowney
Design Manager: Jessica Lowe
Designer: Arielle Gamble
Photographers: Martin Reftel and Jessica Reftel Evans (Amorfo);
    Jessie Wright and Lara Davies
Stylists: Jessie Wright and Lara Davies
Production Manager: Todd Rechner
Production Coordinator: Tessa Spring

Colour reproduction by Splitting Image Colour Studio
Printed in China by 1010 Printing International Limited